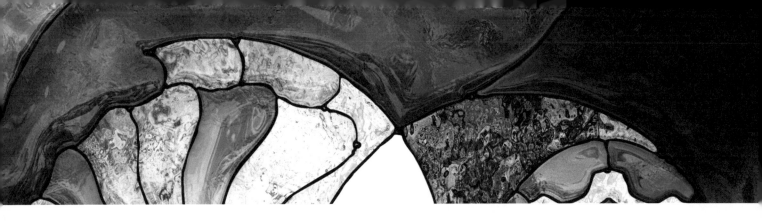

ORACLES IN THE SPHERE

Messages of Divine Oneness

HALLIE LARSSON

Balboa Press books may be ordered through booksellers or by contacting:

Balboa Press
A Division of Hay House
1663 Liberty Drive
Bloomington, IN 47403
www.balboapress.com
1 (877) 407-4847

ISBN: 978-1-9822-1286-5 (sc)
ISBN: 978-1-9822-1285-8 (e)

Print information available on the last page.

Balboa Press rev. date: 11/12/2018

BALBOA.
PRESS
A DIVISION OF HAY HOUSE

ORACLES IN THE SPHERE
Messages of Divine Oneness

HALLIE LARSSON

Acknowledgements

My book would have never gone forward had I not met my dear new friend, book coach and author Nancy Kahalewai. I learned so much from her. She has such patience and organizational skills and we connected so well. She understands these messages of wisdom, and helped guide me through each step of the way. Writing a book and then trying to publish is a whole other language for me. It has been a great experience and fun. I am inspired to create new writings in the near future. Thank you Nancy for all your support, guidance, patience and friendship.

I want to thank my dear friend Lisa Morningstar for her 27-year friendship and support in helping me refine my writings. She really knows how to keep the reader engaged and how to facilitate others in creative and empowering ways. I love her honesty and clarity—she knows me like a book. She was a great sounding board for me as I went through the wonderful journey of manifesting and editing these pages. I feel very blessed to have a friend like Lisa. Thank you Lisa!

I am grateful to all the photographers and artists who rendered these amazing drawings and pictures. And I am so blessed to have my wonderful, creative husband, Stefan. He is my rock, and accepts me unconditionally throughout all my passions and projects.

I remain in deep awe and gratitude to the Universe and Great Spirit within me for guiding me along my path, giving me the love and openness to hear and feel the messages of Divine Oneness. I will continue to listen and be mindful on my journey. May you find your own precious whispers of inspiration within these pages!

"Hallie Larsson's beautiful little book *Oracles in the Sphere* is an invitation to awaken to life's deeper meanings and explore our inner truths. Filled with insights, wisdom and sound spiritual advice—and adorned with evocative photos appropriate to each of her verses—Larsson's book inspires us not only to discover our own unique truths and purposes, but to fully embrace them and put them to use in our lives.

Oracles in the Sphere, however, is not a one-way book meant for passive reading. Larsson invites her readers, stimulated by each verse and picture, to immediately write down their own thoughts, and she provides ample space to do that on each journal page that follows. Those pages include potent questions on topics like how to listen to our intuition and stretch our wings, and what messages we hear from our heart and how to spread our love to the broader world.

Anyone seeking solace, searching for greater purpose, or trying to establish more balance in their life will appreciate this lovely participatory guide to inner exploration."

—Tom Peek, Hawai'i novelist, workshop instructor, and writing mentor

"Hallie Scher Larsson's *Oracles in the Sphere* is packed with luminous messages, and tender words of support and love which open the heart and bath the Soul. We are living in very challenging times and it seems the outside world is a harsh place where anything could happen without notice changing our lives forever. Hallie, with the help of her Spirit Guides, has gifted us with a tool of transformation and inner contemplation, where we can cultivate and nurture our inner landscape, opening and remembering who we are as powerful beings connected to an Infinite Source of Grace.

Hallie and her Guides ask essential questions, encouraging us to write from our own stream of consciousness, diving deep into the wonder and Peace that lies within. Hallie elegantly and simply encourages each one of us to hear the messages of our own Soul and Spirit Guides as we connect to the Oneness of the Universe. She has so much to offer us in this beautiful and inspiring workbook, and I hope that she continues writing and offering us the wisdom of her Spiritual Messages of Light."

—Deb Court, Spiritual Counselor and Travel Guide for John of God, Brazil

Introduction

It was now December 26, 2007, and my spirit within decided that I needed to get these messages out to be heard. I was scared to open this chapter in my life, having never been fond of the public spotlight but at the same time, I knew I had to.

All my life I have felt very different, but who is to say or know what "different" is? As long as I can remember, I have had an inner sense or knowing and wondering about the Universe and the world. I often found myself daydreaming and avoiding what I "should" be doing. I have always been an observer and gifted with strong perceptions. I struggled with my "inner knowing" because of fear of how people would perceive me and my own doubts of who I am.

The Universe is a vastness that is so powerful and far beyond our physical world and comprehension. This spiritual reality is what some call God, the Oneness that every soul is connected to and part of.

I have always been drawn to Spirit, and I just knew and felt in my soul that there was much more to God than what we typically think about. I felt that everything, including human beings, is a part of God's Universe. I always felt there should be no judgment on anyone or anything, yet I fell into worldly thinking. I believed that the human race should love one another and live in harmony, yet I had no idea how we all can reach this level of Oneness.

Since I was a child, I have had various experiences and encounters with angels, entities and 'Aumakua (the Hawaiian concept for our personal guides, ancestors and guardians). I regularly received insightful messages in my meditations, sleep, and when in natural surroundings. They have given me guidance and intrigued me deeply, inspiring me to dig deeper. Yet they have been difficult for me to share with others until this point in my life.

This book has been a long time in the making. I have collected these channeled messages to help me grow, and to help me know my truth and my purpose here on Mother Earth. It is a life journey to understand who we are, and perhaps we will never know, but we still continue to follow the path and gain a deeper understanding of who we are.

I feel that these messages have been told to me to help reveal my own purpose and my personal place in the Universe, and why I am here. I continue to learn from the messages and experiences, and always try to follow the guidance from my knowing heart.

The time is now to share these photos and messages with all of you.

I am not a professional writer or teacher; I'm simply delivering love and light to all beings as it has been delivered to me. I invite you to explore and journey through these messages from what I like to call the Divine Oneness. Enjoy!

We awaken for a moment in time, only to find our truth
within ourselves. We wonder how long have we slept?
We have always had a sense of what was and who we truly
are, before and now. Our deeper inner layers, from time
and time again, unfold from within for us to remember.

Have you ever had the sensation that time stood still or as if time shifted into a feeling of familiarity like a Déjà vu? Pause for that moment. Can you hear the message from your higher self?

We are in each other's lives for many reasons. We guide one another. We watch over one another. We love, understand, feel and touch one another. And, we are inter-connected through many life times.

Who are you expressing the infinite dance with?

Once a butterfly has emerged from his cocoon, he must fly!
There's no reason to go back...

A vast freedom welcomes you.

What can you do today to stretch your wings?
Where will your wings take you?

_____

_____

_____

_____

_____

_____

_____

_____

_____

_____

As you journey along your path, be mindful to walk in your light.

What methods do you use to connect with
your inner wisdom, your light?

_____

_____

_____

_____

_____

_____

_____

_____

_____

_____

_____

Ride the waters to the endless sea!
Sometimes we get stuck and it's hard to keep the flow.
It's natural to go up and down, so don't get discouraged.

What can you do to keep the continuous
flow moving gracefully onward?

_____

_____

_____

_____

_____

_____

_____

_____

_____

_____

_____

Hold your heart in your hands. Look at it very carefully. Feel and hear what it is saying. Know your truth within.

As you reflect upon your heart, can you feel it
speaking to you? What does it say?

_____

_____

_____

_____

_____

_____

_____

_____

_____

_____

_____

Singing birds never sing too loud, for the forest is vast and sound is infinite.

*Beautiful sounds carry, penetrating all who
are listening. What is your song?*

_____

_____

_____

_____

_____

_____

_____

_____

_____

_____

We are here in this moment. Stand with your feet on the ground, while you love laugh smile see cry touch smell! Be here now! Enjoy!

YOU ARE BLESSED!

Can you accept the now? Are you fully present?
If not, where are you?

_____

_____

_____

_____

_____

_____

_____

_____

_____

_____

_____

The smell of the ocean touches our senses, only to give us the taste
of salt on our lips. I yearn to know what is the message in the bottle?
It must have floated far in the deep blue sea,
washing ashore for our heart to see.

The message may be, you are you, I am me, yet together we are we.

Is there a message you are waiting or hoping for?

_____

_____

_____

_____

_____

_____

_____

_____

_____

_____

_____

_____

Give to the Earth and it will nurture your Soul!

Are you planting your seeds and nourishing
one another? How do you give back?

_____

_____

_____

_____

_____

_____

_____

_____

_____

_____

_____

We all have wings! Let Go and Soar!
You can go anywhere you choose. Journey
from here to there ... now deeper with clarity.

Where will your visions take you? What will your new beginnings be?

In the stillness, can you hear me? Can you feel me?
Can you sense me? Touch me?
Embrace me for I am here, with you throughout Eternity.

As above, so below.

How does your intuition speak to you?

_____

_____

_____

_____

_____

_____

_____

_____

_____

_____

_____

_____

_____

Sometimes we can just visit and daydream.
Unplug!
Let your mind go; give yourself permission to rest and Just Be.

What stories have the clouds shared with you?

_____

_____

_____

_____

_____

_____

_____

_____

_____

_____

_____

_____

_____

Let me in when I come knocking on your door! We are one soul together, here and now. Like a plant, our roots are so deep, they flow through us like an underground stream. Know I am here with you always. Keep your door open!

Can you imagine your higher self being rooted in eternity?
What are the ways you connect to your higher self?

_____

_____

_____

_____

_____

_____

_____

_____

_____

_____

_____

There are days we are not ourselves: the scales are off balance.
We have eyes and ears, yet we cannot see nor hear.
We feel uncertainties when detached from our inner knowing.
When the tide has gone out,
remember it always comes back to the shores it knows best...
Your inner YOU!

Every moment of every day can be a balancing act.
What brings you in balance?

_____

_____

_____

_____

_____

_____

_____

_____

_____

_____

_____

Gleaming seas—pounding, engulfing.
You have touched my world; can I touch yours?
You swim in the depths of the blue ocean.
Can I get to know you?

Where's your connection with these grand creatures?

_____

_____

_____

_____

_____

_____

_____

_____

_____

_____

_____

_____

Hello! I'm here. Like a soft breeze, I pass over your body, gently touching your face.

Can you feel the gentle reminders that Love is everywhere? What reminds you of this?

_____

_____

_____

_____

_____

_____

_____

_____

_____

_____

_____

_____

Complete
light and love
can provide
Justice for all
Nations.

See the light around all nations—beyond borders. We are all part of humanity. How do you see beyond our differences?

Sometimes we live in two worlds, not knowing how to balance our soul. Parts of us want to go one way, other parts tug at us to go the other way. We are so complex, our minds full of thoughts, questions and needs. Sometimes knowing and sometime not, our past and future are often uncertain.

If we stay patient, breathe deeply, and take one day at a time, the answers will come from within.

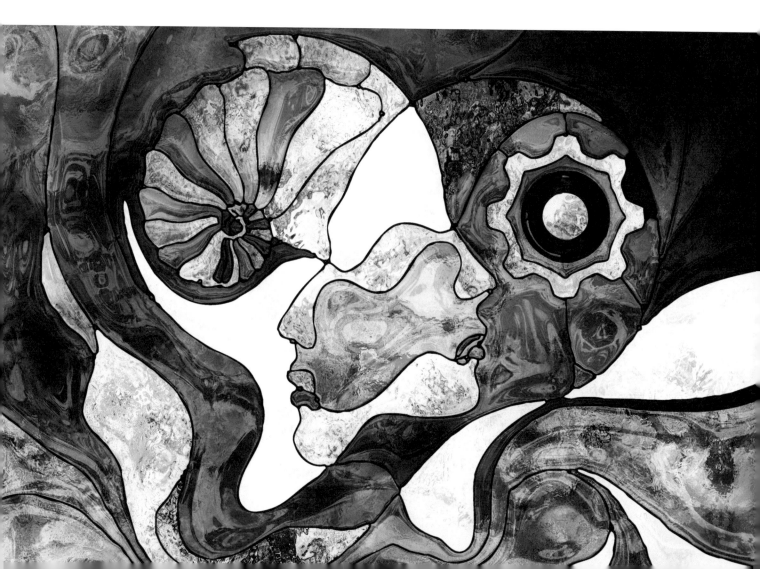

Have faith! Keep all options open. How can you align yourself in the Divine Oneness so the answers come?

_____

_____

_____

_____

_____

_____

_____

_____

_____

_____

_____

Touch the water,
for while it is water,
it is also you!
We are
interconnected—
with the clouds,
rain, rivers, oceans.

We are One.

What are the ways you feel connected to water and the other elements?

The real treasures and gifts are found within.

You are the pot of gold! You are a rainbow light being!
What are the gems about you that make your light shine?

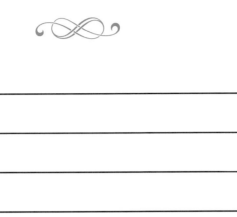

_____

_____

_____

_____

_____

_____

_____

_____

_____

_____

_____

Whisper a secret to the wind,
and it shall blow a kiss for you!

Like little seeds, what can you do to spread your love to the world?

_____

_____

_____

_____

_____

_____

_____

_____

_____

_____

_____

_____

_____

As I awaken, what is my heart feeling?
An energy force flows though my body,
like I have only felt once before.
Encompassing, pulsating. At times it frightens me,
but I get a sense to just let go.
I flow with it; I can feel a bright energy.

Energy, light and love permeate my being, and I am not afraid.
Bright empowering light forces joined together,
for a few moments in time.
Fading ever so slowly, as I fall back to sleep.
It felt so real, so wonderful, where did it come from?

Can you feel the glory? What special moments
have touched you like that?

_____

_____

_____

_____

_____

_____

_____

_____

_____

_____

_____

When the heart is open and unlimited, it hears
life's music and dances to its love songs.

What love songs do you dance to?

_____

_____

_____

_____

_____

_____

_____

_____

_____

_____

_____

_____

Paint the sky with the color of your blue eyes,
the forest and mountains with the color of your green eyes,
and the deserts with your brown eyes.
The beauty of our world is seen
with the eyes that are able to perceive.

You can paint the world any color you want.
What colors and pictures are on your canvas?

_____

_____

_____

_____

_____

_____

_____

_____

_____

_____

_____

Mahalo nui (thank you very much) for joining my journey into Divine Oneness! I will be sharing my amazing stories and personal journeys in 2019 and beyond, which I truly feel will be empowering and inspirational for all of you who resonate with these messages and insights. I humbly invite your comments and participation in the next chapters of our lives ahead as we continue to evolve and navigate our life journeys, and truly appreciate any book orders or events you may want to extend to me.

Aloha! – Hallie

Please eMail me at: contact@oraclesinthesphere.com
Or simply visit my page and contact me online
via: www.OraclesInTheSphere.com

Printed in the United States
By Bookmasters